My STORy

A Kid's Creative Journal for Expressing Yourself

Janine Wilburn

WEST
MARGIN
PRESS

My Name

My name is joy

My name is the light in my family's eyes

My name is what I hear when I succeed

My name is what I hear when I fail

My name is not common

My name is not strange

My name is who I am

My name has its own special story

My name is _____

This journal belongs to

_____

We can bring a heart of understanding and compassion to a world that needs it so much.

—Jack Kornfield

#

INTRODUCTION

This journal is all about you! This book is about having fun while writing about your life. You are the author and the main character, so tell your story your way and create what you want your life to look like. This book is also filled with information and tools that will help you learn how to handle tough times. It will teach you how to recover quickly from difficulties and challenges by being strong, flexible, and positive—by being resilient.

What is resilience? Resilience is the ability to deal with the hard stuff in a positive way for you. For example, resilience helps you deal with someone being mean, or problems at home, or stress at school. It also helps you deal with all the stuff that comes with growing up. Resilient people can deal with the most difficult experiences and come out on the other side even stronger.

So, why should you care? Being resilient makes life easier and more fun, while also helping you stay calmer and less upset when things get difficult. Being resilient helps you achieve your dreams as you have the strength to never give up, and resilience is something you will use for the rest of your life.

How to Use This Book

This journal helps by asking you questions about your life now and your dreams for the future. Use words or drawings to fill in the prompts and to answer questions. Remember, this is your story and you are in charge, so add anything you'd like to any page.

Have a good time filling in the blanks, drawing pictures, imagining and creating cool things—all of which will help build your resilience.

Here are some things to think about as you get started with this journal:

- The person you most admire...
- If you had a magic wand, how you would use it...
- Your favorite family moment...
- The silliest thing you ever did...
- The planet you would like to visit...
- Who you dream of becoming...

Today you are You, that is truer than true. There is no one alive who is Youer than You.

—Dr. Seuss

ABOUT ME

THIS IS ME

This is your story. Close your eyes and take three slow, deep breaths. Now pick up your pen or pencil to write and draw with, and get started creating your book.

My birthday is _____

I was born in _____

I go to school at _____

I live in _____

THIS IS ME

My favorite toy is/was _____
_____

A funny story about me when I was younger is:
_____
_____
_____
_____

What I like most about being a kid is:
_____
_____
_____
_____

I first realized that I was growing up when:
_____
_____
_____
_____

THIS IS ME

My room looks like _____

_____

_____

I share it with _____

It is the color of _____

Here is a drawing or photo of my room:

PLACES I LOVE

These are my special places, where I like to go to hang out and relax.

In my house:

Outside my house:

In my neighborhood:

PEOPLE I ADMIRE

When I was little, I looked up to:

-
-
-

My heroes were:

-
-
-

I loved these heroes because:

_____

_____

_____

_____

PEOPLE I ADMIRE

Now I look up to:

-
-
-

I'd like to be like:

-
-
-

My real-life heroes are:

_____

_____

_____

_____

IN MY IMAGINATION

If I could live in a book or movie, it would be

_____ because:

If I could be a character from a book or movie, it would

be _____ because:

IN MY IMAGINATION

Draw or write your answers below, whatever feels most comfortable for you.

If I had a magic wand, I would create:

If I had a magic wand, this is what I would change:

IN MY HEART

Fill these pages with your heart's desires. Close your eyes and think of six things you wish would come true. Then draw them or write about them here.

WISH ONE
   I wish:

WISH TWO
   I wish:

WISH THREE
   I wish:

WISH FOUR
  I wish:

WISH FIVE
  I wish:

WISH SIX
  I wish:

Happiness is not something ready-made. It comes from your own actions.

—Dalai Lama [Tenzin Gyatso]

MY HAPPINESS TRACKER

Happiness Tracking

In this section, have fun thinking about people, places, and things that make you feel content, peaceful, good, joyful—happy! Then draw and write about them. This way you can have something to go read later to remind yourself of those wonderful moments. On days when you are feeling a little down, rereading what you write in this section will help you feel better.

I FEEL MY HAPPINESS HERE

Close your eyes and think about something that makes you very happy. Then notice where the happiness lives in you. Mark and color the places here.

This special space is a place for you to draw or write what happiness feels like to you.

PEOPLE & THINGS THAT MAKE ME SMILE

Smiling isn't just fun—it also makes you feel good! Fill out the list with your top ten choices of people and things that make you smile.

1) _____

2) _____

3) _____

4) _____

5) _____

6) _____

7) _____

8) _____

9) _____

10) _____

PEOPLE & THINGS THAT MAKE ME LAUGH

Sometimes smiles can lead to laughter. Write down the people and things that make you laugh!

_____ makes me laugh.

_____ makes me laugh.

_____ makes me laugh.

_____ makes me laugh.

_____ makes me laugh.

I laughed so hard about _____

I laughed so hard about _____

I laughed so hard about _____

I laughed so hard about _____

I laughed so hard about _____

PEOPLE & THINGS I CARE ABOUT

Think about the people and things that are really important to you, and then write them down below.

I really care about _____

I really care about _____

I really care about _____

I really care about _____

I really care about _____

I really care about _____

I really care about _____

I really care about _____

I really care about _____

I really care about _____

PEOPLE & THINGS THAT HELP ME FEEL CARED ABOUT

What makes you feel warm and cozy and loved? Fill in the blanks below with all the people and things that make you feel special and cared about.

_____ really cares about me.

_____ really cares about me.

_____ really cares about me.

_____ really cares about me.

_____ really cares about me.

I feel cared about when _____

I feel cared about when _____

I feel cared about when _____

I feel cared about when _____

I feel cared about when _____

PEOPLE & THINGS
I HAVE HAPPY MEMORIES ABOUT

Draw or write about people and events that you want to remember.

-
-
-
-
-

PEOPLE & THINGS
I HAVE HAPPY MEMORIES ABOUT

-
-
-
-
-

MY TOP FIVE MOVIES

List your five favorite movies below and write what you like most about each movie.

1) _____

What I like most about it:

_____

2) _____

What I like most about it:

_____

3) _____

What I like most about it:

_____

4) _____

What I like most about it:

_____

5) _____

What I like most about it:

_____

MY TOP FIVE BOOKS

List your five favorite books below and write what you like most about each book.

1) _____

What I like most about it:

_____

2) _____

What I like most about it:

_____

3) _____

What I like most about it:

_____

4) _____

What I like most about it:

_____

5) _____

What I like most about it:

_____

MY FAVORITE SHOWS, VIDEOS, OR GAMES

Name your favorite TV shows, YouTube videos, board games, video games, podcasts, and everything else. You can list them in any order you like.

MY FAVORITES

WHY I LIKE IT

1) _____   _____

2) _____   _____

3) _____   _____

4) _____   _____

5) _____   _____

6) _____   _____

7) _____   _____

8) _____   _____

9) _____   _____

10) _____   _____

MY FAVORITE FOODS

Fill in the circles with the names, drawings, or photos of your favorite foods. Then write what you like most about them. Is it the smell? The memories the food brings up? Or maybe it's the taste or specific flavor?

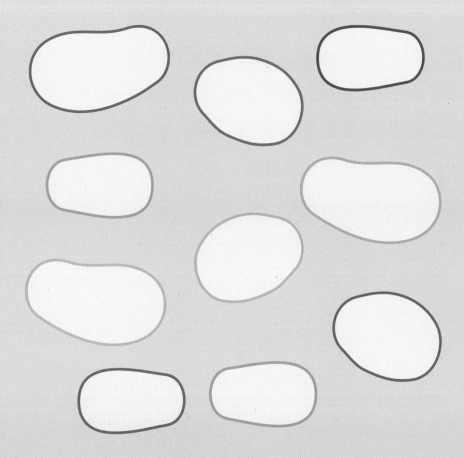

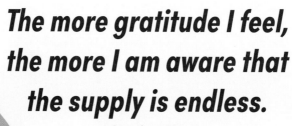

The more gratitude I feel,
the more I am aware that
the supply is endless.
—Louise Hay

USING THE
GRATITUDE TOOL

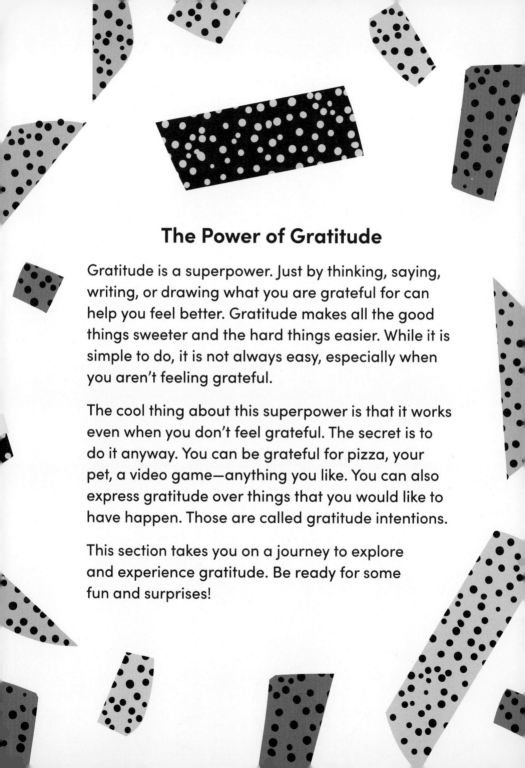

The Power of Gratitude

Gratitude is a superpower. Just by thinking, saying, writing, or drawing what you are grateful for can help you feel better. Gratitude makes all the good things sweeter and the hard things easier. While it is simple to do, it is not always easy, especially when you aren't feeling grateful.

The cool thing about this superpower is that it works even when you don't feel grateful. The secret is to do it anyway. You can be grateful for pizza, your pet, a video game—anything you like. You can also express gratitude over things that you would like to have happen. Those are called gratitude intentions.

This section takes you on a journey to explore and experience gratitude. Be ready for some fun and surprises!

MY GRATITUDE LIVES HERE

Close your eyes and think about something you are grateful to have in your life. Then notice where the gratitude lives in you. Mark and color the places here.

This special space is a place for you to draw or write what gratitude feels like to you.

PEOPLE I AM GRATEFUL TO HAVE IN MY LIFE

On this special page, write the name of family members and friends you are grateful to have in your life. Write each name in a color that reminds you of that person.

♥ _____   ♥ _____

♥ _____   ♥ _____

♥ _____   ♥ _____

♥ _____   ♥ _____

♥ _____   ♥ _____

♥ _____   ♥ _____

♥ _____   ♥ _____

♥ _____   ♥ _____

♥ _____   ♥ _____

♥ _____   ♥ _____

PEOPLE I AM GRATEFUL TO HAVE IN MY LIFE

On this special page, write the name of **classmates**, **teachers**, **coaches**, neighbors, and mentors you are grateful to have in your life. Write each name in a color that reminds you of that person.

◆ _____   ★ _____

◆ _____   ★ _____

◆ _____   ★ _____

◆ _____   ★ _____

◆ _____   ★ _____

◆ _____   ★ _____

◆ _____   ★ _____

◆ _____   ★ _____

◆ _____   ★ _____

◆ _____   ★ _____

IN MY EVERYDAY LIFE, I AM GRATEFUL FOR...

Gratitude is an inspiring way to start or end your day. For the next week, write down at least three things you are grateful for every day.

Writing daily gratitude lists helps you become more resilient. On those really hard days, you can read and reread your already written gratitude statements to help you feel better. Gratitude is most powerful when you do it every day.

MONDAY

I am grateful for _____

I am grateful for _____

I am grateful for _____

TUESDAY

I am grateful for _____

I am grateful for _____

I am grateful for _____

WEDNESDAY

I am grateful for _____

I am grateful for _____

I am grateful for _____

THURSDAY

I am grateful for _____

I am grateful for _____

I am grateful for _____

FRIDAY

I am grateful for _____

I am grateful for _____

I am grateful for _____

SATURDAY

I am grateful for _____

I am grateful for _____

I am grateful for _____

SUNDAY

I am grateful for _____

I am grateful for _____

I am grateful for _____

SPECIAL TIMES & MEMORIES
I AM GRATEFUL FOR

Fill in the blanks on these pages with people, things, and events that make you feel good!

I am grateful for _____

I am grateful for _____

I am grateful for _____

I am grateful for _____

I am grateful for _____

I am grateful for _____

I am grateful for _____

I am grateful for _____

I am grateful for _____

I am grateful for _____

SPECIAL TIMES & MEMORIES
I AM GRATEFUL FOR

I am grateful for _____

I am grateful for _____

I am grateful for _____

I am grateful for _____

I am grateful for _____

I am grateful for _____

I am grateful for _____

I am grateful for _____

I am grateful for _____

I am grateful for _____

GRATITUDE INTENTIONS

Here is a special space to write things you would like to have happen in your life. For each line, write each gratitude as if the thing you'd like has already happened. For example, if you want a bicycle, you would write: *I am grateful for my new bike*. Then read these pages a lot, especially on days when you feel sad, mad, or disappointed.

I am grateful for _____

I am grateful for _____

I am grateful for _____

I am grateful for _____

I am grateful for _____

I am grateful for _____

I am grateful for _____

I am grateful for _____

I am grateful for _____

I am grateful for _____

GRATITUDE INTENTIONS

Imagine how you would like your family, friends, and school to be. Now write your gratitude for those things.

I am grateful for _____

I am grateful for _____

I am grateful for _____

I am grateful for _____

I am grateful for _____

I am grateful for _____

I am grateful for _____

I am grateful for _____

I am grateful for _____

I am grateful for _____

When you carry out acts of kindness you get a wonderful feeling inside. It is as though something inside your body responds and says, yes, this is how I ought to feel.

—Harold Kushner

THE VALUE OF KINDNESS

Kindness

Kindness is a gift that can be easily given and received every day. It can be as simple as a smile at a teacher, a check-in on a classmate, or a quick text to a friend. Each of these efforts takes only a few minutes, but they have the power to change someone's day, including your own day.

Whether you are extending or accepting a helping hand, the warmth, happiness, and even joy are always present. So, share yourself and your kindness—you will feel better!

MY KINDNESS LIVES HERE

Kindness can come in many forms, through actions, thoughts, words, and more. Close your eyes and think about a time in your life when you were kind to someone or when someone was kind to you. Then notice where the kindness lives in you. Mark and color the places here.

This special space is a place for you to draw or write what kindness feels like to you.

DAILY ACTS OF KINDNESS

Writing down acts of kindness will make you feel good. Fill in the blanks here with acts of kindness you have done for others, as well as kind things others have done for you. For example, you could write: *Today I was kind to my friend when I told them they looked really good.*

Today I was kind to _____
when I _____

Today I was kind to _____
when I _____

Today I was kind to _____
when I _____

Today _____ was kind to me when
_____

Today _____ was kind to me when
_____

Today _____ was kind to me when
_____

DAILY ACTS OF KINDNESS

Today I was kind to _____
when I _____

Today I was kind to _____
when I _____

Today I was kind to _____
when I _____

Today I was kind to _____
when I _____

Today _____ was kind to me when
_____

Today _____ was kind to me when
_____

Today _____ was kind to me when
_____

Today _____ was kind to me when
_____

KINDNESSES I WILL ALWAYS REMEMBER

Throughout your life there are special kindnesses that you received and will always remember.

These pages are places to keep those memories. Write what you remember and draw how you felt then or how you feel now reliving that memory.

KINDNESSES I WILL ALWAYS REMEMBER

You will know that forgiveness has begun when you recall those who hurt you and feel the power to wish them well.

—Lewis B. Smedes

PRACTICING FORGIVENESS

Forgiveness

Forgiveness is an incredibly powerful tool that is often misunderstood. People might think forgiveness is a gift given to someone who has hurt or harmed them in some way. But forgiveness is really a gift to the person doing the forgiving, because it allows that person to move on. This helps the person let go of the hurt and unhappiness.

Think about it. When we forgive someone who hurt us, we are refusing to let the hurt continue. Forgiveness allows us to release the anger and upset that we might be holding onto, and then we can heal. We can let go and move on.

MY FORGIVENESS LIVES HERE

Take a deep breath and think about a time when someone forgave you for something you did and wish you hadn't done. Then take another deep breath and think about a time when you forgave someone for something they had done to you. Notice where you feel forgiveness and color the places where forgiveness lives in you.

This special space is a place for you to draw or write what forgives feels like to you.

This important space is just for you. Write down anything you want to forgive yourself for. We all do things that later we wish we didn't do. Learning to forgive ourselves is the first step in learning how to forgive.

I forgive myself for _____

I forgive myself for _____

I forgive myself for _____

I forgive myself for _____

I forgive myself for _____

I forgive myself for _____

I forgive myself for _____

I forgive myself for _____

I forgive myself for _____

I forgive myself for _____

Write down everyone you forgive for embarrassing you, making you cry, or hurting you or your feelings. This page is just for you. It is up to you whether you share your forgiveness statements with anyone or just keep them to yourself. The important part is to honestly forgive the person so you can let go of the upset.

I forgive _____ for _____

I forgive _____ for _____

I forgive _____ for _____

I forgive _____ for _____

I forgive _____ for _____

I forgive _____ for _____

I forgive _____ for _____

I forgive _____ for _____

I forgive _____ for _____

I forgive _____ for _____

There is no such thing as too much forgiveness, so here is another page to fill in if you need it.

I forgive _____ for _____

I forgive _____ for _____

I forgive _____ for _____

I forgive _____ for _____

I forgive _____ for _____

I forgive _____ for _____

I forgive _____ for _____

I forgive _____ for _____

I forgive _____ for _____

I forgive _____ for _____

This page is about the people you hope will forgive you for doing or saying something that you wish you could take back.

I hope _____ forgives me for
_____

I hope _____ forgives me for
_____

I hope _____ forgives me for
_____

I hope _____ forgives me for
_____

Draw a picture of how you feel after doing some forgiveness.

You can't use up creativity.
The more you use,
the more you have.
—Maya Angelou

FINDING CREATIVITY

Creativity

This section is full of fun things for you to do. These are the kinds of things you do just because you feel like it. This section has ideas and projects to get your imagination going—then comes the creative boost! It is important to remember to just engage in the project, not worry about how it is going to turn out. The final product doesn't matter—it is being creative that lifts you up.

Now close your eyes for a minute, take a deep breath, and let your imagination go. Complete each page by yourself or with your family and friends. Keep these pages to yourself or share them. It's all up to you. Just have fun and enjoy the energy!

WHERE MY CREATIVITY LIVES

Close your eyes and think about something you made or created. It can be a game, a song, a drawing, an invention, a cake, cookies—really, anything that you made up. Then notice where the creativity lives in you. Mark and color the places here.

This special space is a place for you to draw or write what creativity feels like to you.

WHERE WOULD I GO?

If you could time travel, where would you go and who would you take with you? Draw or write your answers on these pages.

THE BEST SUPERPERSON EVER

Use your imagination to create a very special SUPERPERSON—your superperson! What is their name and what do they look like? Draw a picture of them.

Name _____

THE BEST SUPERPERSON EVER

List your superperson's superpowers. Begin the list with their very special power, a power that only they have and the one they use the most.

★ _____

★ _____

★ _____

★ _____

★ _____

★ _____

★ _____

★ _____

★ _____

★ _____

THE AWARD GOES TO...

Create and present your very own awards! It is up to you to decide what and who to recognize with a trophy or ribbon. For example, give the Congratulations Ribbons and Trophies for achievements like the Funniest Storyteller, Best PB&J Maker, Kindest Gesture, and Most Awesome Friend. It is all up to you!

THE IMPORTANCE OF SINGING & DANCING

Make a list of seven songs that you like a lot, then assign each song to a day of the week. For every day of the week, sing that song and dance to it however you like. Feel free to change the song whenever you want. Just make sure to sing and dance to at least one song a day.

SUNDAY'S SONG: _____

MONDAY'S SONG: _____

TUESDAY'S SONG: _____

WEDNESDAY'S SONG: _____

THURSDAY'S SONG: _____

FRIDAY'S SONG: _____

SATURDAY'S SONG: _____

THE IMPORTANCE OF SINGING & DANCING

Now draw a picture of what you feel like each day after you sing and dance to the song you chose.

SUNDAY

THURSDAY

MONDAY

FRIDAY

TUESDAY

SATURDAY

WEDNESDAY

*I found that if you love life,
life will love you back.*

—Arthur Rubinstein

FUN TIMES

All about Fun

Laughter, joy, silliness, and play make life more fun, and fun makes life more inspiring. Fun is good for our hearts, our heads, and our bodies. This section will ask you to recognize fun in your life and to do things to generate more of it. Fun is good—and good for you!

WHERE FUN LIVES IN ME

Close your eyes and think about a
time when you really had fun—when
you smiled, laughed, and felt really
comfortable while doing something.
Now notice where the fun lives in you.
Mark and color the places here.

This special space is a place for you to
draw or write what creativity feels like to you.

EVERYDAY FUN

It is important to have some fun every day! List below the fun things you like to do.

For fun, every day I like to _____

For fun, every day I like to _____

For fun, every day I like to _____

For fun, every day I like to _____

For fun, every day I like to _____

For fun, every day I like to _____

For fun, every day I like to _____

For fun, every day I like to _____

For fun, every day I like to _____

For fun, every day I like to _____

FUN FACTS

The funny thing about fun is that it is not always easy.
List below things that are hard but fun for you to do.

★ _____

★ _____

★ _____

★ _____

★ _____

★ _____

★ _____

★ _____

★ _____

★ _____

A FUN TIME

Tell a story of a time you had a lot of fun when you didn't expect to. Write about what you thought was going to happen and then how it changed. How did the fun show up?

_____

_____

_____

_____

_____

_____

_____

_____

_____

_____

_____

_____

_____

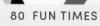

THE SILLIEST THINGS I'VE EVER DONE

Being silly is part of having fun! Being silly can also make you feel better when you are feeling a little sad or upset. On this page, write down the silliest things you've done that you had fun doing.

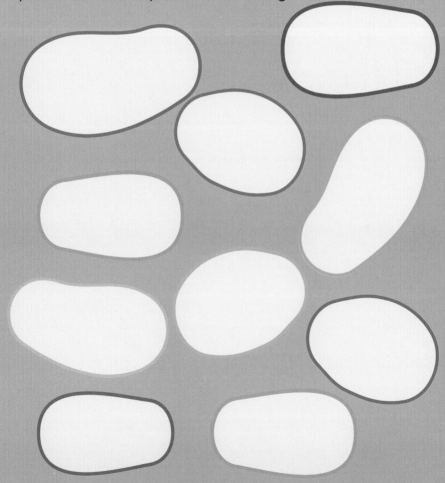

MY TOP FIVE MOST FUN MOMENTS EVER

In order of the most fun, write or draw about the most fun you have ever had.

MY #1 MOST FUN TIME EVER:

MY #2 MOST FUN TIME EVER:

MY #3 MOST FUN TIME EVER:

MY #4 MOST FUN TIME EVER:

MY #5 MOST FUN TIME EVER:

When we seek to discover the best in others, we somehow bring out the best in ourselves.

—William Arthur Ward

INSIDE SCOOP
ON MY FAMILY

THIS IS MY FAMILY

These are names of everyone I consider my family and their relationship to me.

NAME	RELATIONSHIP
_____	_____
_____	_____
_____	_____
_____	_____
_____	_____
_____	_____
_____	_____
_____	_____
_____	_____
_____	_____
_____	_____
_____	_____
_____	_____
_____	_____
_____	_____

THIS IS MY FAMILY

Use this space to draw or glue photographs of your family members.

ALL ABOUT MY FAMILY

My first family memory is:

My family is the best at:

What is unique about my family is:

My family inspires me to:

I am proud of my family because:

What I have learned about my family is:

ALL ABOUT MY FAMILY

The most important thing I have learned about life from my family is:

The funniest story about my family is:

Check off special activities that your family likes to do together. If it is not on the list, then add it.

- ☐ Cook dinner together
- ☐ Watch our favorite sports
- ☐ Go hiking
- ☐ Go shopping
- ☐ Laugh
- ☐ Play games
- ☐ Go out for ice cream
- ☐ Eat dinner together
- ☐ Watch movies
- ☐ _____
- ☐ _____

I especially love it when we _____ because:

ALL ABOUT MY FAMILY

Our family traditions are:

Our family holidays are:

My favorite holiday is:

I like it best because:

Too often we underestimate the power of a touch, a smile, a kind word, a listening ear, an honest compliment, or the smallest act of caring, all of which have the potential to turn a life around.

—Leo Buscaglia

IMPORTANT
MOMENTS
IN MY LIFE

MY MOMENTS

There are times, moments, and events in your life that you will remember forever. Fill these pages with those special memories. Then you can come back and reread them when you need a little boost.

PROUD MOMENTS

The bravest thing I ever did was:

I had the courage to do it because:

I knew I was growing up when:

LEARNING MOMENTS

The most important lesson I've learned about life is:

I learned it when:

The second most important lesson I've learned about life is:

I learned it when:

The third most important lesson I've learned about life is:

I learned it when:

FIRST-TIME MOMENTS

The first time I went to school was:

I remember feeling:

The first time I played any sport was:

I liked it or did not like it because:

The first time I was NOT treated like a little kid was:

I felt:

The first time I went somewhere alone was:

I felt:

GRADUATION MOMENTS

Graduations are times of transition. They mark the passage from one accomplishment to a new set of challenges at the next level. Reflect on your graduation days and write down what you remember from those important days in your life.

I graduated from _____
On that day, I remember feeling:

I graduated from _____
On that day, I remember feeling:

I graduated from _____
On that day, I remember feeling:

What I think it will feel like to graduate from high school:

MY MOST IMPORTANT DAY

Use this page to tell the story about what you feel is the most important day you've had in your life up to now.

The most important day of my life so far is:

_____

_____

_____

_____

_____

_____

_____

_____

_____

_____

_____

_____

Ordinary people believe only in the possible. Extraordinary people visualize not what is possible or probable, but rather what is impossible. And by visualizing the impossible, they begin to see it as possible.

—Cherie Carter-Scott

WISDOM
TO LIVE BY

KNOWLEDGE TO REMEMBER

A big part of growing up is learning something new all the time about different kinds of things. There is the learning in school, learning about other people, learning about taking care of yourself, learning to help others—and the list goes on and on. This section helps you identify the most useful information you have learned about life so far. This information is often referred to as wisdom.

THE BEST ADVICE

The best advice I received was:

This is how I use that advice:

This is how I feel when I use the advice:

THE PEOPLE I ADMIRE

The person or people I look up to the most are:

-
-
-
-
-

The most important people in my life are:

-
-
-
-
-

THE MOST INSPIRATIONAL PEOPLE

Here are some of the people who inspired me to be my best self and how they did it.

The teacher who inspired me the most is:

_____

How they did it:

_____

_____

The coach or instructor who inspired me the most is:

_____

How they did it:

_____

_____

Other people who inspire me:

-

-

-

-

THE MOST INSPIRATIONAL PEOPLE

If I could meet anybody I wanted to, I would choose to
meet _____ because

_____

I would ask them about:

_____

_____

My favorite person from history is:

_____

_____

I admire them because:

_____

_____

The question I want to ask them is:

_____

_____

Remember there's no such thing as a small act of kindness.

—Scott Adams

HELPING
OTHERS

WHAT I CAN DO

Helping others is an amazing experience because when you give from the heart, you receive just as much in return. Helping others provides you with a purpose that brings you joy and fulfillment even when you are feeling down.

HOW I FEEL WHEN I HELP SOMEONE

Take a deep breath and think about a time when you helped someone or when someone helped you. Notice how you felt when you helped others, then circle the words below that best describe your feelings. Feel free to add more words if you want.

HAPPY   **Joyful**   VALUABLE

Like I make a difference

Warm-hearted   *Like dancing*

Important   THOUGHTFUL   **Healthy**

COMPASSIONATE   KIND   Sensitive

I CAN HELP

If I could help one person do something they really want to do, I would help _____
to do _____
because _____
_____
_____
_____

My best contribution to another person was:
_____
_____
_____
_____
_____

More people I can contribute to include:
_____
_____
_____
_____
_____

OTHER WAYS I CAN HELP

Think about some other ways that you can help or be of service, and write your ideas down on these pages.

At home, I could help out by:

At school, I could help out by:

After-school activities I could participate in to help others are:

OTHER WAYS I CAN HELP

Clubs and organizations I could join that focus on contributing to others are:

I could volunteer at:

New ideas I have about ways I can help others are:

*So many of our dreams
at first seem impossible,
then they seem improbable, then,
when we summon the will,
they soon become inevitable.*

—Christopher Reeve

MY DREAMS
FOR THE FUTURE

I CAN PICTURE IN MY MIND

This section helps you create what you'd like your life to look like when you grow up. Use your creativity and brilliance to imagine the world as you would like it to be, as well as what you would like to be doing. Once you can imagine it, you have started on your path.

In my future, I imagine there will be:

_____

_____

_____

_____

_____

_____

_____

_____

_____

_____

I will travel to:

-

-

-

-

I want to travel because:

-

-

-

-

I want to learn to:

-

-

-

-

MY PASSIONS

I love to _____

I'd like to become a _____
because _____
_____
_____
_____

I think I will be good at _____
because _____
_____
_____
_____

I've always secretly wished I could:
_____
_____
_____
_____

MY ACCOMPLISHMENTS

I think my greatest talent is:

I believe I can:

I want to be known for:

MY PLANS

I think that success is when you:

I want to contribute to others by:

MY PLANS

Check off and add to the list below of what you want to
do in the future.

IN THE FUTURE, I WANT TO:

□ Finish high school

□ Go to College

□ Travel

□ Join the military

□ Get a job

□ Celebrate

□ Hang my diploma on the wall

□ _____

WHEN I AM OLDER, I WANT TO:

□ _____

□ _____

□ _____

□ _____

□ _____

MY HOPES

The most important day in my whole life will be when:

One thing I am committed to changing is:

I am going to change it by:

MY HOPES

This is how I wish the world was different:

I wish it was different because:

My one wish for all the people of the world is:

Resilience

Joy... balance... light and laughter,

Sunlight... water... bright with love,

*Ability to be yourself in
the face of challenge*

Flexible strength.
—J. Wilburn

This journal never really ends. It is made for you to keep nearby and look at whenever you need a pick-me-up, a boost, or something to smile or laugh about. It is also a reminder to continue to do the activities that help build your resilience, confidence, and strength.

Check off the tools you enjoyed most as a reminder to use them. Then pick your favorite activity and try to do it every day for at least one month, and then the next month, and then the next month...

☐ Filling out my daily happiness tracker
☐ Making daily gratitude lists
☐ Recording daily acts of kindness
☐ Writing down daily acts of forgiveness
☐ Creating something every day
☐ Making sure I do at least one fun thing every day
☐ Helping someone else every day

My favorite activity that I commit to doing every day is

_____

beginning on this date: _____.

ACKNOWLEDGMENTS

My deepest gratitude to everyone recognized here, who without their support I would never have undertaken the Resiliency Guide series. First, my family, my family is always first. Thank you for your unshakable belief in my healing, and for believing that I could write these journals even with my health limitations. Knowing you were there for me at every twist and turn made it possible for me to fulfill my dream of sharing this life-altering information with as many people as possible. I am so grateful.

Thank you to all my teachers during this 24-year healing journey. I am truly at a loss for words to describe the depth of my appreciation for you always being there to instruct and assist me. To my yoga teacher, you took me on as a student when I could barely move at times. I will always remember the dignity and respect with which you treat me as I continue to study yoga and work on my recovery. To Pam Lanza & Glenn Hirsch who helped me find, connect, acknowledge, and own both my inner and outer artist when I didn't know I had either. I miss you both, may you rest in peace. To Dr. Maud Nerman for teaching and role modeling that healing is a lifelong journey and to never give up.

I am grateful for my many friends and colleagues who stood with me during these challenging years, enthusiastically encouraging my writing, art, and innovations. My dear friend Faith Winthrop who told me this was going to happen, I will celebrate with you in my heart. I am grateful for Aiko Morioka and Cathy River who provided wise, compassionate counsel as I wrote these books. I am grateful for my oldest friend Laurie McFarlane for being there for me for 40 years. Thank you to Glenn Hartelius, Rick Ackerly, Gordon Sumner, Karen Leveque, and Matt Schwartz for supporting me in so many different ways. I also want to thank the many people around the world who trust me with their joys, fears, accomplishments, hurts, and their hearts. I am honored to be of service to you!

Thank you to those of you who literally these books would not exist without your stellar work. To Luke Schwartz, research assistant extraordinaire for expanding and coordinating my 20-plus years of research sources. To the amazing team at West Margin Press, I am so grateful to all of you. To Jen Newens for understanding my vision and providing the platform for this information to reach so many others. To Olivia Ngai for your detailed, precise, and tireless editing. To Rachel Metzger for your thoughtful, innovative designs and your open collaboration. Angie Zbornik for your strategic marketing ideas, innovative execution, and support. I deeply appreciate each and every one of you. Thank you!

ABOUT THE AUTHOR

Janine Wilburn is an award-winning artist, innovator, and writer. She has a master's degree in East West Psychology and is pursuing her PhD. For decades, Janine worked as a marketing professional, receiving recognition for her work with a Cannes Film Festival Bronze Lion, a Clio, and other awards, until a car accident changed her life. Suffering spinal damage, she needed to heal. Through her studies in neuroscience, neuroplasticity, yoga, and meditation, Janine persevered and developed resilience-building practices. The Resiliency Guides are the result of her research, experience, hope, and commitment to help others. Janine lives in San Francisco, California.

I dedicate this journal to my son, Christian. Your limitless resilience and boundless creativity inspire me every day.

Art Credits: MURRIRA / Shutterstock.com; LHF Graphics / Shutterstock.com; AlexHliv / Shutterstock.com

ISBN: 9781513267326

Printed in China
1 2 3 4 5

Published by West Margin Press®

WEST
MARGIN
PRESS
WestMarginPress.com

Proudly distributed by Ingram Publisher Services

WEST MARGIN PRESS
Publishing Director: Jennifer Newens
Marketing Manager: Angela Zbornik
Project Specialist: Micaela Clark
Editor: Olivia Ngai
Design & Production: Rachel Lopez Metzger